PARASAUROLOPHUS

BY REBECCA SABELKO

EPIC

BELLWETHER MEDIA • MINNEAPOLIS, MN

EPIC BOOKS are no ordinary books. They burst with intense action, high-speed heroics, and shadows of the unknown. Are you ready for an Epic adventure?

This edition first published in 2021 by Bellwether Media, Inc.

No part of this publication may be reproduced in whole or in part without written permission of the publisher. For information regarding permission, write to Bellwether Media, Inc., Attention: Permissions Department, 6012 Blue Circle Drive, Minnetonka, MN 55343.

Library of Congress Cataloging-in-Publication Data

Names: Sabelko, Rebecca, author.
Title: Parasaurolophus / Rebecca Sabelko.
Description: Minneapolis, MN : Bellwether Media, 2021. | Series: Epic : The world of dinosaurs | Includes bibliographical references and index. | Audience: Ages 7-12 | Audience: Grades 4-6 |
Summary: "Engaging images accompany information about the parasaurolophus. The combination of high-interest subject matter and light text is intended for students in grades 2 through 7"-- Provided by publisher.
Identifiers: LCCN 2020014877 | ISBN 9781644872932 (library binding) | ISBN 9781681038384 (paperback) | ISBN 9781681037561 (ebook)
Subjects: LCSH: Parasaurolophus--Juvenile literature.
Classification: LCC QE862.O65 S239 2021 | DDC 567.914--dc23
LC record available at https://lccn.loc.gov/2020014877

Editor: Betsy Rathburn   Designer: Jeffrey Kollock

Printed in the United States of America, North Mankato, MN

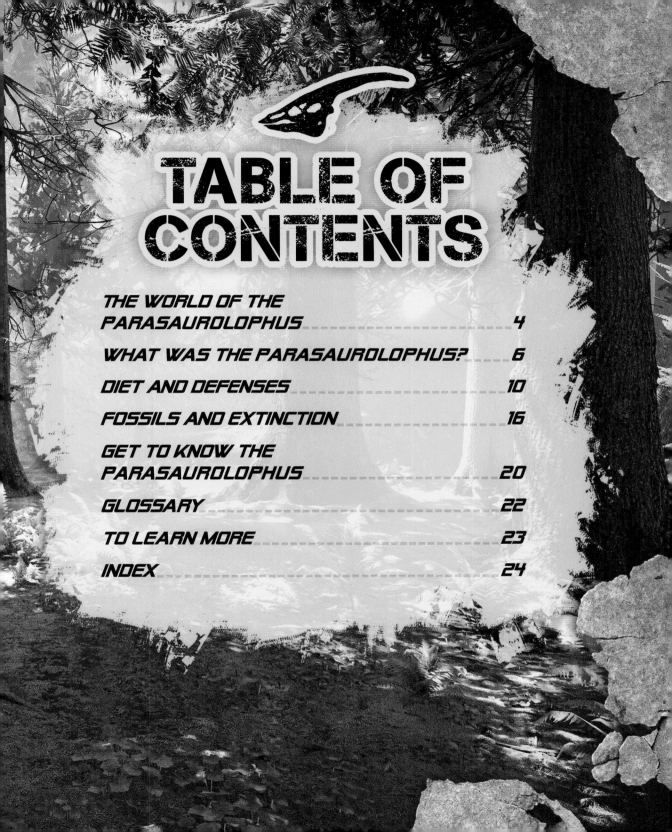

TABLE OF CONTENTS

THE WORLD OF THE PARASAUROLOPHUS

The parasaurolophus is famous for the long **crest** on top of its head.

The dinosaur roamed Earth around 75 million years ago during the Late **Cretaceous period**. This was during the **Mesozoic era**.

Late Cretaceous period

crest

par-ah-SAWR-OL-uh-fus

WHAT WAS THE PARASAUROLOPHUS?

young parasaurolophus

The parasaurolophus was a **hadrosaur**. Its mouth looked like a duck beak.

THE BIGGEST CREST!

The parasaurolophus had the biggest crest of any hadrosaur. It grew up to 6 feet (2 meters) long!

Its crest was long and hollow. Air moved through the crest to make a loud sound. The dinosaur sounded like an elephant!

The parasaurolophus was big! It reached up to 36 feet (11 meters) in length. It weighed up to 8,000 pounds (3,629 kilograms). Small, round scales covered its body.

SIZE CHART

15 feet (4.6 meters)

10 feet (3 meters)

5 feet (1.5 meters)

DIET AND DEFENSES

The parasaurolophus ate many tough plants. It walked on four legs as it ate plants from the ground.

It stood on its back legs
to reach high leaves.

PARASAUROLOPHUS DIET

leafy plants

tree leaves

ferns

The parasaurolophus used its toothless beak to gather plants into its mouth.

beak

⚠ **ADVANCED TEETH!**

Some scientists believe hadrosaurs had some of the most complex teeth that have ever evolved!

The dinosaur's jaw had a **dental battery**. The strong battery was used to grind up tough plants.

This hadrosaur did not have many defenses against enemies. It gathered in groups for safety.

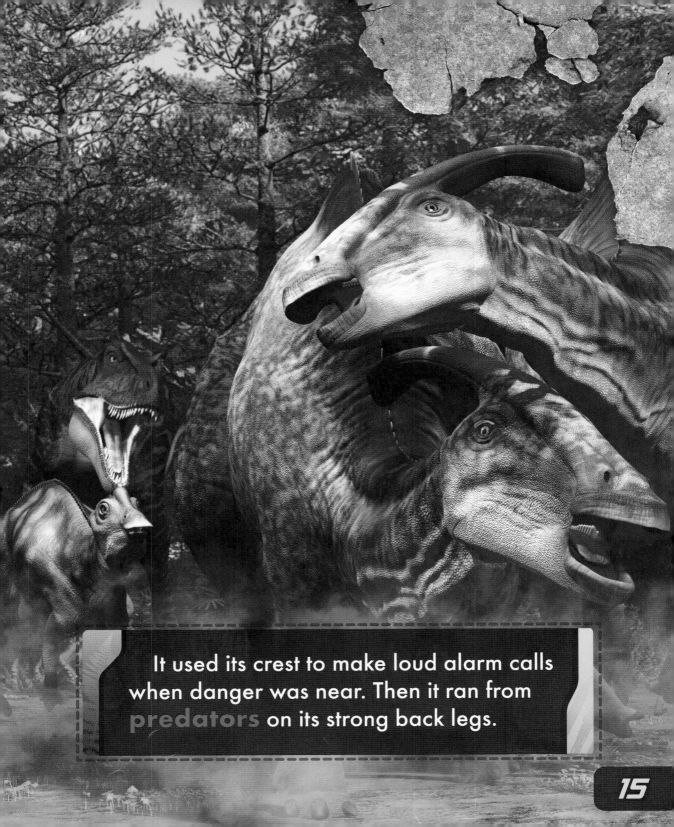

It used its crest to make loud alarm calls when danger was near. Then it ran from **predators** on its strong back legs.

FOSSILS AND EXTINCTION

Earth began to cool at the end of the Late Cretaceous period. Some plants and animals began to **evolve**.

The parasaurolophus could not survive the changes. The dinosaur went **extinct**.

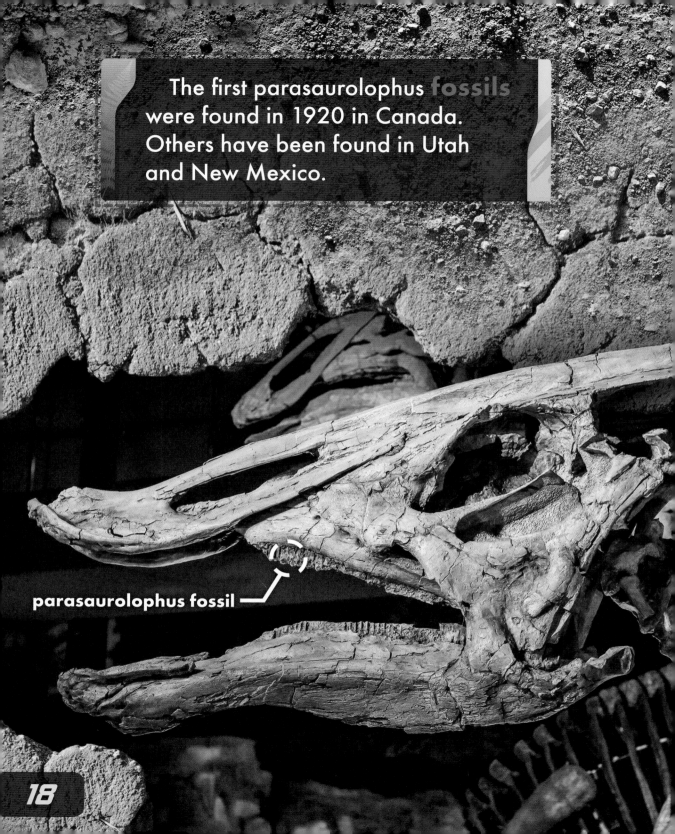

The first parasaurolophus fossils were found in 1920 in Canada. Others have been found in Utah and New Mexico.

parasaurolophus fossil

PARASAUROLOPHUS FOSSIL MAP

Canada

United States

Mexico

KEY

⟶ fossil site

Scientists use the fossils to learn about this dinosaur. They may discover more in the future!

GET TO KNOW THE PARASAUROLOPHUS

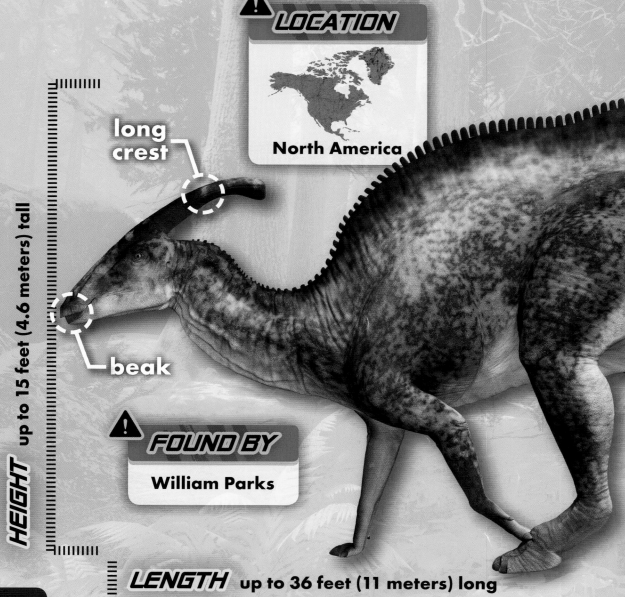

LOCATION

North America

long crest

beak

HEIGHT up to 15 feet (4.6 meters) tall

FOUND BY

William Parks

LENGTH up to 36 feet (11 meters) long

100 million to 66 million years ago during the Late Cretaceous period

Mesozoic era

| Triassic | Jurassic | Cretaceous |

⚠️ **FIRST FOSSILS FOUND**

Alberta, Canada, in 1920

⚠️ **FOOD**

leafy plants

ferns

strong back legs

⚠️ **WEIGHT**

up to 8,000 pounds (3,629 kilograms)

GLOSSARY

crest—a showy growth on the head of an animal

Cretaceous period—the last period of the Mesozoic era that happened between 145 million and 66 million years ago; the Late Cretaceous period began around 100 million years ago.

dental battery—a group of hundreds of tightly packed teeth that work together to grind tough plants

evolve—to change slowly, often into a better, more complex state

extinct—no longer living

fossils—the remains of living things that lived long ago

hadrosaur—a type of dinosaur from the Late Cretaceous period that often had a crest on its head, a beak, and a jaw filled with grinding teeth; hadrosaurs are often called duck-billed dinosaurs.

hollow—empty through the middle

Mesozoic era—a time in history in which dinosaurs lived on Earth; the first birds, mammals, and flowering plants appeared on Earth during the Mesozoic era.

predators—animals that hunt other animals for food

TO LEARN MORE

AT THE LIBRARY

Braun, Eric. *Could You Survive the Cretaceous Period?: An Interactive Prehistoric Adventure.* North Mankato, Minn.: Capstone Press, 2020.

Clark, Mike. *Parasaurolophus.* New York, N.Y.: Kidhaven Publishing, 2018.

Kelly, Tracey. *Tyrannosaurus and Other Cretaceous Dinosaurs.* Tucson, Ariz.: Brown Bear Books, 2018.

ON THE WEB

FACTSURFER

Factsurfer.com gives you a safe, fun way to find more information.

1. Go to www.factsurfer.com.

2. Enter "parasaurolophus" into the search box and click 🔍.

3. Select your book cover to see a list of related content.

INDEX